The Fine Lines Journal

44 Meditations for Intentional Living

Julianne Victoria

© 2018 by Julianne Victoria and Through the Peacock's Eyes Press

www.peacockseyes.com

All Rights Reserved

No part of this book may be used or reproduced in any manner what-so-ever, including internet usage, without written permission of Julianne Victoria except in the case of properly referenced brief quotations embodied in articles and reviews.

Julianne Victoria

Julianne Victoria

Introduction

I came up with the idea for *The Fine Lines* in the early 2000's when I really began to observe both myself and those around me very closely. What I noticed were the often very subtle, yet very significant differences in behaviors, including ways of thinking, feeling, and being, that greatly affect how we create our lives. So I started jotting down these subtly different behaviors and meditated on the fine lines that separated them. Over the years I would add to the list and I have now come up with 44 simple, yet profound, meditations. It is my hope that by spending time meditating, contemplating, and journaling on these fine lines, we will embark on a journey of self-discovery that can lead us from conditional living to intentional living.

In Gratitude,

Julianne Victoria

Julianne Victoria

Contents

1. Acceptance vs Settling
2. Act of Kindness vs Action for Reward
3. Aspire vs Desire
4. Assertiveness vs Aggression
5. Awareness vs Ignorance
6. Being vs Seeking to Be
7. Being Present vs Being a Bystander
8. Busy vs Overwhelmed
9. Child-like vs Childish
10. Compassion vs Pity
11. Consciousness vs Intellect
12. Courage to Take Action vs Forcing Something to Happen
13. Destiny vs Fate
14. Discernment vs Judgement
15. Discipline vs Habit
16. Ecstacy vs Obsession
17. Empathy vs Sympathy
18. Exploring Solutions vs Dwelling on Problems
19. Faith vs Belief
20. Give & Receive vs Give & Take
21. Gratitude vs Indebtedness
22. Heart-centered vs Mind-centered
23. I Am You vs You Are Me
24. Imagination vs Fantasy
25. In Love vs In Lust
26. Inspiration vs Impulse

27. Intuition vs Instinct
28. Joy vs Pleasure
29. Love vs Fear
30. Non-conformist vs Rebel
31. Private vs Secretive
32. Pushing Through vs Getting Lost In
33. Responding vs Reacting
34. Responsibility vs Paranoia
35. Retreat vs Escape
36. Self-Confidence vs Arrogance
37. Self-Empowerment vs Self-Denial
38. Solitude vs Loneliness
39. Sovereignty vs Dominance
40. Supporting vs Controlling
41. Surrender vs Giving Up
42. Teaching vs Telling
43. Vulnerability vs Victimhood
44. Why? vs Why Me?

On Versus

In the notebook in which I had begun to write down these fine lines, I had used the abbreviation for the word *versus (vs)* to represent the fine line between the two words or concepts whose subtle differences I was contemplating. In everyday speech we use the word *versus* to mean something is against or battling against some other thing, such as in sports. For example: the home team versus the away team. Looking back now, knowing where I was on my personal journey, I probably thought of it in that way – as if one word or term was the favored or "good" one and the other was the opposed or "bad" one. However, I have come to understand that these fine lines were fine not because the two concepts were separate from or battling with each other, but because they were often the two sides of the same coin. Each of the two sides creates the contrast that allows us to see the other side.

Some of the fine lines are less subtle and more commonly viewed as opposites, such as **Love vs Fear**. For others the fine lines are almost invisible, such as **Joy vs Pleasure**. Yet, whether clear or blurry, we must view the fine lines not as barriers, boundaries, or separators, but as the connecting points where we meditate and contemplate on the contrast between the two terms. By doing so we begin to turn into ourselves to grow, to change, and to transform. We realize that it is not one against the other, but one *is* because of the other's existence. It's versus *and* vice versa! Like the yin-yang symbol, each is a part of the other in a continual interlocking spin. With this understanding we can begin to appreciate both sides of the fine lines.

The word *versus* comes from the past participle of the Latin verb *vertō, vertere,* which means in its transitive form: *to turn (something), to transform (something), and to change (something).* In its intransitive form it means: *to turn oneself, to be transformed, and to be changed.* It is my hope that the following 44 Fine Lines inspire you to turn within and transform yourself as you meditate, contemplate, and journal upon them. May you embark on a journey of self-discovery that leads you from living conditionally to living intentionally.

1. ACCEPTANCE VS SETTLING

2. ACT OF KINDNESS
VS
ACTION FOR A REWARD

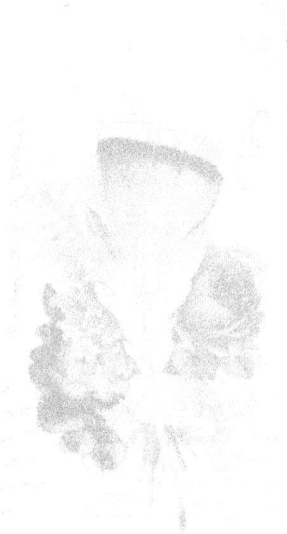

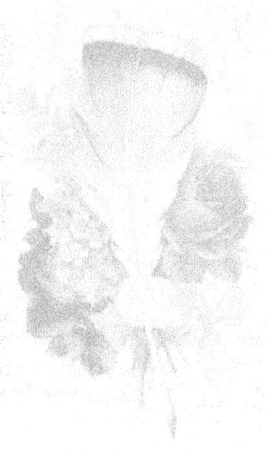

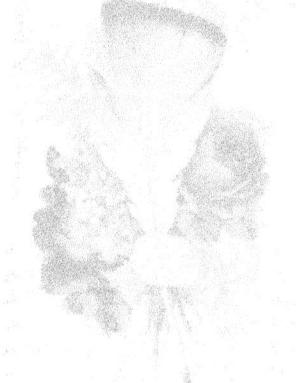

3. ASPIRE VS DESIRE

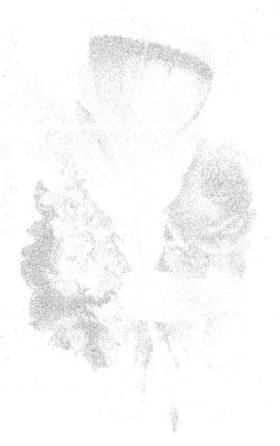

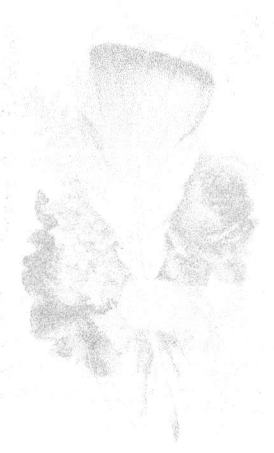

4. ASSERTIVENESS VS AGGRESSION

5. AWARENESS VS IGNORANCE

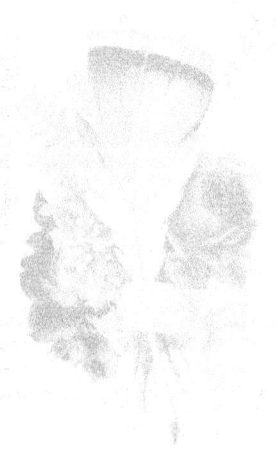

6. BEING VS SEEKING TO BE

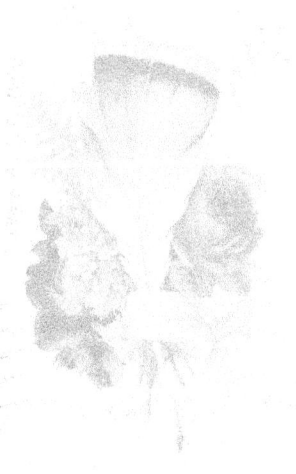

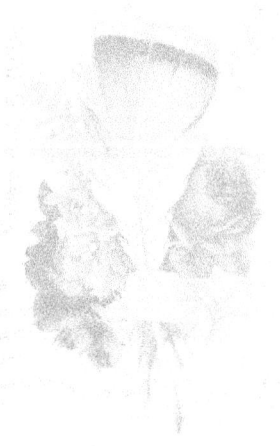

7. BEING PRESENT VS BEING A BYSTANDER

8. BUSY VS OVERWHELMED

9. CHILD-LIKE VS CHILDISH

10. COMPASSION VS PITY

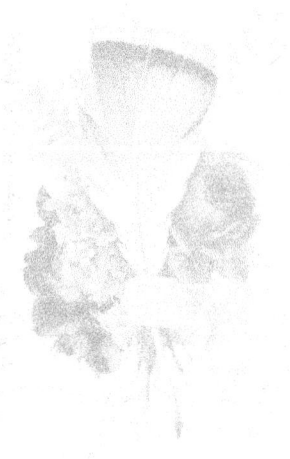

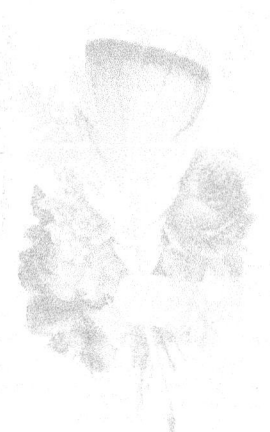

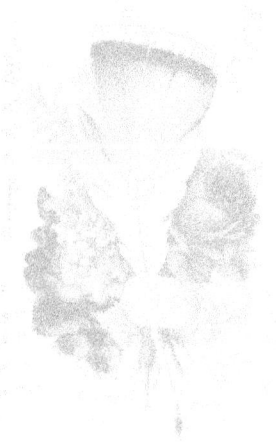

11. CONSCIOUSNESS VS INTELLECT

12. COURAGE TO TAKE ACTION VS FORCING SOMETHING TO HAPPEN

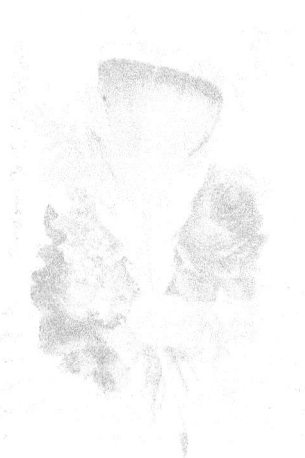

13. DESTINY VS FATE

14. DISCERNMENT VS JUDGEMENT

15. DISCIPLINE VS HABIT

16. ECSTACY VS OBSESSION

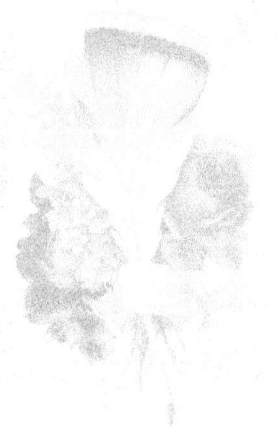

17. EMPATHY VS SYMPATHY

18. EXPLORING SOLUTIONS
VS
DWELLING ON PROBLEMS

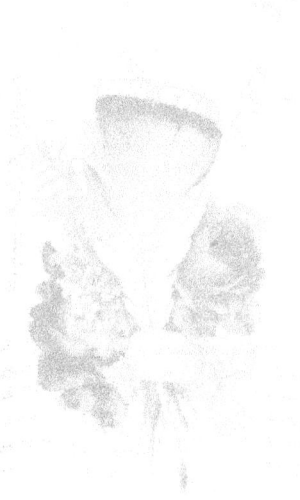

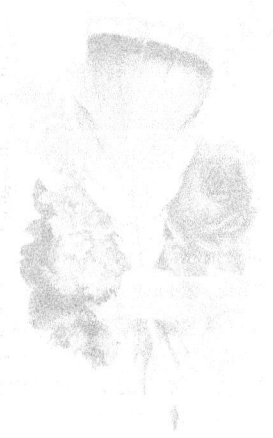

19. FAITH VS BELIEF

20. GIVE & RECEIVE VS GIVE & TAKE

21. GRATITUDE VS INDEBTEDNESS

22. HEART-CENTERED VS MIND-CENTERED

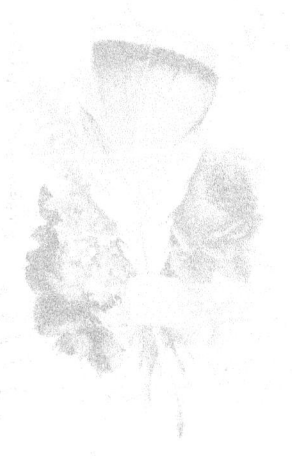

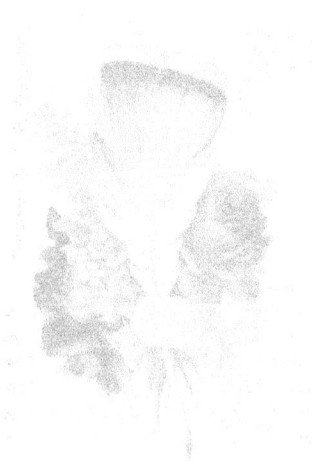

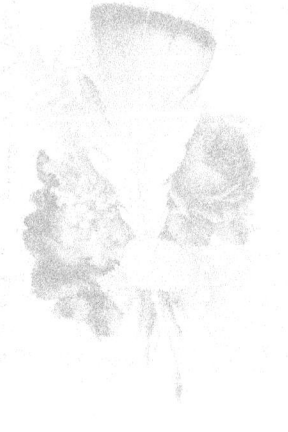

23. I AM YOU VS YOU ARE ME

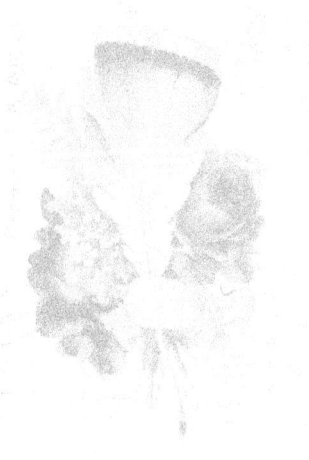

24. IMAGINATION VS FANTASY

25. IN LOVE VS IN LUST

26. INSPIRATION VS IMPULSE

27. INTUITION VS INSTINCT

28. JOY VS PLEASURE

29. LOVE VS FEAR

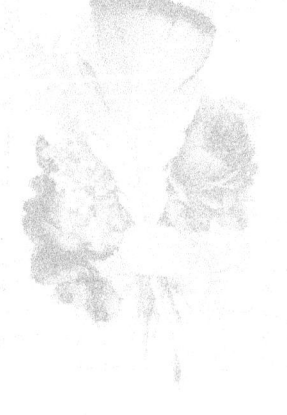

30. NON-COMFORMIST VS REBEL

31. PRIVATE VS SECRETIVE

32. PUSHING THROUGH
VS
GETTING LOST IN

33. RESPONDING VS REACTING

34. RESPONSIBILITY VS PARANOIA

35. RETREAT VS ESCAPE

36. SELF-CONFIDENCE VS ARROGANCE

37. SELF-EMPOWERMENT
VS
SELF-DENIAL

38. SOLITUDE VS LONELINESS

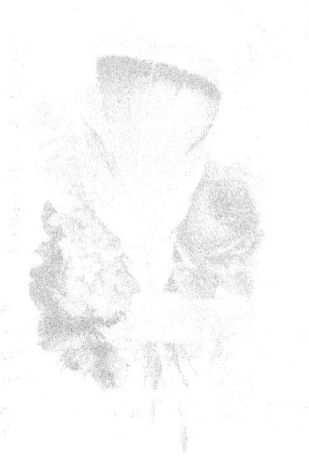

39. SOVEREIGNTY VS DOMINANCE

40. SUPPORTING VS CONTROLLING

41. SURRENDER VS GIVING UP

42. TEACHING VS TELLING

43. VULNERABILITY VS VICTIMHOOD

44. WHY? VS WHY ME?

ABOUT THE AUTHOR

Julianne Victoria is a writer, spiritual life coach, and intuitive healer. It is her hope to inspire, teach, and guide others on their journeys in this life.

www.juliannevictoriacoaching.com
www.peacockseyes.com

www.ingramcontent.com/pod-product-compliance
Lightning Source LLC
Chambersburg PA
CBHW070135100426
42743CB00013B/2704